Life Stories
Shakespeare

Marcella Forster

Illustrated by David McAllister

WAYLAND

Life Stories

Louis Braille

Christopher Columbus

Grace Darling

Guy Fawkes

Anne Frank

Gandhi

Helen Keller

Martin Luther King

Nelson Mandela

Florence Nightingale

Shakespeare

Mother Teresa

Cover and title page photograph: The famous portrait of Shakespeare by Chandos.
Cover illustration: An Elizabethan street scene in front of the Globe Theatre

Editor: Polly Goodman
Designer: Joyce Chester

First published in 1995 by
Wayland (Publishers) Ltd
61 Western Road, Hove
East Sussex BN3 1JD, England

British Library Cataloguing in Publication Data
Forster, Marcella
Shakespeare. – (Life Stories)
I. Title
II. Series
822.33

ISBN 0 7502 1619 0

Typeset by Joyce Chester, England
Printed and bound in Italy by G. Canale and C.S.p.A., Turin

Contents

Words in **bold** are explained in the glossary on page 30.

A healthy boy

It was a bright April day in Stratford-upon-Avon, Warwickshire, in the year 1564. The sun was shining down on the busy little town, and people were hurrying to the market to do their shopping.

In a big house in Henley Street, Mary Shakespeare lay in bed, sweating and groaning. She was about to have her third baby. But Mary was worried.

The house in Stratford-upon-Avon where William Shakespeare was born.

Many babies did not survive in those days and her first two babies had died. A wave of pain gripped her. She let out a roar, gave a big push and the baby was born. It was a little boy. Mary and her husband, John, decided to call their son William. They prayed that this child would live.

That year, the **plague** swept through England. The deadly disease, carried by rats' fleas, killed 200 people in Stratford. Luckily for the Shakespeares, little William survived.

Young Will

William soon had two brothers and two sisters, Gilbert, Richard, Joan and Anne. His father, John Shakespeare, was a glove maker and his mother had **inherited** some farmland and money. So his family was quite well off.

William's father worked at home making fine leather gloves. He sold them on his stall under the clock-tower in Stratford marketplace. His business was successful and the townspeople admired him.

When William was four, the townspeople made his father High Bailiff of Stratford. This was a bit like being the mayor and it made William's father very important in the town. He wore a red robe with fur on it when he went to the town's big **events**.

One of William's father's jobs was to give **licences** to actors who were visiting the town. These allowed the actors to put on their plays and the Shakespeares went to see the performances. William was thrilled by the excitement of the plays.

William and his father watch a play put on in the open air. ▼

7

▲ The top floor of this building was the grammar school where William was a pupil.

School-days

Only boys went to school in Shakespeare's time. William's first school was Petty School, where he learned to read and write. Around the age of seven, he went to the grammar school in Stratford. There he learned Latin and studied the Bible and history. In the top classes, no one was allowed to speak English. They had to speak in Latin, which is the old language of the Romans.

The school day was very long and tiring. William started school at 6 am and didn't finish until 5 pm. He had to go to school six days a week and did not get many holidays. When the boys were naughty, they were hit with a **birch-rod**. One boy carved this complaint in Latin on a desk: 'Nothing comes from working hard.'

▲ The grammar school had just this one classroom.

When William was twelve, his father suddenly had money problems. So William had to leave school to help his father with the glove business.

9

Marriage and children

When William was eighteen, he met Anne Hathaway, the daughter of a farmer. Anne lived about a kilometre away from William, across the fields in the village of Shottery. She was twenty-six years old. Anne and William were married in November 1582.

▲ Anne Hathaway's cottage.

Anne moved into William's parents' house in Stratford. In May 1583, she gave birth to their first child, Susanna. Two years later Anne had twins, a boy called Hamnet and a girl called Judith. By the age of twenty-one, William was the father of three children.

Shortly after the twins were born, William left Stratford. His wife and children stayed behind. No one knows why William left or where he went. Some say he went to work for a **lawyer**. Others think he became a teacher. One story says he was caught poaching Sir Thomas Lucy's deer from Charlecote Park near Stratford and had to run away to London.

William leaves Anne and the twins in Stratford. ▼

London and the theatre

Sometime between 1585 and 1592, William arrived at the gates of the city of London. He looked around in amazement. Huge ships were sailing up the River Thames into the heart of the walled city. Up above him, **traitors'** heads were stuck on poles on London Bridge Gate. Horses' hooves clattered through the narrow streets, and laughter spilled from the busy inns.

William decided to stay. He found himself **lodgings** and set out to look for work.

▲ London in Shakespeare's time, with London Bridge in the centre of the picture. You can see the traitors' heads over the gate at this end of the bridge.

12

William soon decided to work in the
theatre. There were lots of jobs to do –
sweeping the floor, reminding the
actors when to go on stage, and
looking after people's horses while
they watched the plays.

Going to the theatre was very different from today. It was a bit like going to a football match. Plays were only put on in the daytime. People started to queue early in the day. It cost one penny to stand round the stage, and twopence for a seat and a roof over your head. Rich people paid to sit on balconies.

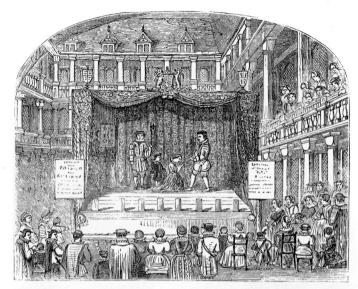

▲ A theatre company puts on a play in an inn yard.

While the **audience** waited for the play to start, they chatted to their friends. They bought **ale** and nibbled nuts and apples. Sometimes a **cutpurse** would sneak through the crowd stealing purses. If he was caught, he was tied up on stage during the **interval** and the crowd threw apple cores at him.

Outside the theatre a woman sells apples and a cutpurse tries to steal money. ▼

William loved watching the plays. There were tales from the Bible, battles from history, love stories and **comedies**.

The stage was huge, and the audience was very close to the actors. The actors came on to the stage through a door at the back and wore beautiful costumes.

▲ A theatre in Shakespeare's time. People paid more to sit on the balconies.

Drums rolled, trumpets called, lightning flashed and cannon roared. Some actors hid **bladders** full of pigs' blood and animal guts under their shirts. When they were 'stabbed' during the play, the bladders burst and spilt blood and guts all over the stage.

It was so exciting that William decided to become an actor and to write his own plays. He was enjoying life in London, but he missed his family. So once a year he went home to Stratford to visit them.

William reminds actors of their words. ▶

16

A successful playwright

The plays William wrote were very popular. Huge crowds queued to see the bloodthirsty play *Titus Andronicus*. In this play, Titus's daughter is attacked by some men who are brothers. Titus catches the brothers, cuts them up and puts them in a pie. Then he feeds the pie to their mother!

A scene from
Henry VI. ▼

Shakespeare's play *Henry VI* was such a success that it was put on fifteen times at the Rose Theatre in one year.

William (sitting in the centre) and some other famous men of his time. Sitting behind William is his friend Ben Jonson, who was also a playwright.

Most of the other successful **playwrights** in London, like Christopher Marlowe, had been to **university**. William had not, and many people looked down on him because of this. But it did not stop him from becoming successful.

The plague

Carts full of dead to bury.

◀ In 1592, the plague swept through London's overcrowded slums, killing 10,000 people.

In 1592 the plague struck London. The theatres were closed to stop the disease spreading through the audience crowds. While they were shut, William wrote a poem called *The Rape of Lucrece* for the Earl of Southampton. Some people say the young earl paid William £1,000 for the poem.

▼ The Earl of Southampton.

Then William wrote 154 beautiful poems called sonnets. He wrote the sonnets for his friends, but soon everyone wanted to read them.

In 1594 the theatres opened again. William gave up writing poetry and went back to his plays. He worked very hard, writing two or three plays a year and acting in many more.

While the theatres were closed, Christopher Marlowe had been stabbed in a fight in a London inn. William's greatest **rival** was dead.

▲ Christopher Marlowe.

William got the ideas for his plays from old stories, poems and real events. His plays made audiences laugh, and cry, and gasp in horror.

A Midsummer Night's Dream is a very funny play. William probably wrote it for a wedding that Queen Elizabeth I went to. In this play, a naughty fairy puts a magic love potion on Queen Titania's eyes while she is asleep. The potion will make her fall in love with the first person she sees when she wakes up. The first person Titania sees is a poor weaver called Bottom. He looks very silly because he is wearing a donkey's head.

▲ Scenes from *A Midsummer Night's Dream.* ▼

William's play *Romeo and Juliet* is one of the most famous love stories in the world. Romeo and Juliet fall in love, but their families hate each other and will not let them marry. So the young lovers plan to run away. But the plan goes wrong and the couple end up killing themselves.

A royal favourite

The Globe Theatre. ▶

William carried on acting as well as writing. He belonged to a group of actors called the Lord Chamberlain's Men. They often acted at Queen Elizabeth's **court.** The queen liked Falstaff in William's play *Henry IV*. So he wrote another play about Falstaff, *The Merry Wives of Windsor,* specially for her.

By the time William was thirty-three, he was making a lot of money and was famous. He bought New Place, the second-biggest house in Stratford, and went there often to visit his family. Gradually he bought more and more land. Then he bought a share in London's finest theatre, the Globe. It was on the south bank of the River Thames and was made of wood.

Queen Elizabeth I loved watching Shakespeare's plays. ▼

24

When Queen Elizabeth I died in 1603, James I became king. He ordered William's company to change its name to the King's Men. The group often acted at the king's court, and William wrote *Macbeth* specially for King James. The King's Men were asked to entertain at the wedding of King James's daughter. One month they put on a total of fourteen plays.

▲ King James I of England.

In June 1613, William's play *Henry VIII* was put on at the Globe Theatre. During the play, a cannon shot out a burning paper ball. It landed on the thatched roof of the theatre. Soon the whole building was on fire. Within an hour it was burnt to the ground.

The final years

After the fire at the Globe Theatre in 1613, Shakespeare decided to **retire** from work and return to Stratford to be with his family. He was forty-nine years old and had written thirty-seven plays. His daughters, Susanna and Judith, had both grown up and married, but his son, Hamnet, had died.

▲ New Place, in Stratford.

In 1616 William wrote his will. He left most of his land and property to his family. He also left money to the poor people of Stratford. But his greatest treasure, his writing, was left for the whole world to enjoy.

William died on 23 April 1616 at the age of fifty-two. He was buried two days later in Holy Trinity Church. On his gravestone is a warning that he might have written himself:

*'Blessed be the man that
 spares these stones
And cursed be he that
 moves my bones.'*

▲ Shakespeare's monument, in Holy Trinity Church, Stratford.

Glossary

ale Beer.

audience A group of people who watch a play.

birch-rod A bundle of twigs or a stick from a birch tree, used to hit someone.

bladders Thin bags of skin or other material that are easily stretched by the liquid or air inside them.

comedies Funny plays.

court A king or queen's home and their attendants.

cutpurse An old word for a pickpocket or thief. People did not have pockets in Shakespeare's time. Thieves stole money from people by taking their purses.

events Important things that happen, such as plays or concerts.

inherited Passed down by a relative who has died.

interval A break in the middle of a play.

lawyer A person who is an expert in the law.

licences Pieces of paper giving permission for something.

lodgings A rented room in another person's house.

plague A deadly disease, caught from the bites of rats' fleas, which spreads quickly through crowds.

playwrights People who write plays.

retire To give up a regular job or profession.

rival A person who is in competition with another person.

traitors People who have helped their country's enemy.

university A place for higher education after school.

Date chart

1564 Shakespeare is born in Stratford-upon-Avon.
1582 Marries Anne Hathaway.
1583 Daughter Susanna is born.
1585 Twins, Hamnet and Judith, are born.
1585–92 Shakespeare moves to London.
1592 The plague. Theatres close in London.
1593 Christopher Marlowe dies.

1594 Theatres open again.
1597 Shakespeare buys New Place, in Stratford.
1603 Queen Elizabeth I dies. James I becomes King of England.
Lord Chamberlain's Men change their name to the King's Men.
1613 The Globe Theatre burns down. Shakespeare retires to Stratford.
1616 Shakespeare dies.

Books to read

Great Lives: William Shakespeare by Dorothy Turner (Wayland, 1985)
Shakespeare, the Animated Tales: Twelfth Night abridged by Leon Garfield (Heinemann, 1992)
Shakespeare for Everyone: Hamlet by Jennifer Mulherin (Cherrytree Press, 1988)
Shakespeare for Everyone: Macbeth by Jennifer Mulherin (Cherrytree Press, 1988)
Shakespeare for Everyone: Romeo and Juliet by Jennifer Mulherin (Cherrytree Press, 1988)

Index

The publishers would like to thank the following for allowing their photographs to be used in this book: Ben Christopher/Performing Arts Library 22; Mary Evans *Cover,* Title page, 14; Michael Holford 12; Hulton Deutsch 19, 20 (bottom), 21; Jarrold Publishing 9, 10, 28, 29; National Portrait Gallery 26; Topham 5, 8, 20; Wayland Picture Library 16, 24.